*THE TRAVELING*
*CONSULTANT'S GUIDE*

TO

# AUDITING ORACLE DATABASE 10G AND 11G

First Edition

The Traveling Consultant's Guide to Auditing Oracle Databases

First Edition

Printed in the United States of America

First Printing: March, 2012

ISBN-978-1-105-62145-1

# CONTENTS

# Introduction

The primary reason for this handbook is that I found that there are not many checklists out there for *auditing* Oracle databases, and the ones that do exist don't really focus on securing the data. Checklists are good, but to a point. In many cases, solutions are not nearly as simple as they are made out to be.

When auditing Oracle databases (and other IT environments), it is important to understand the data flow, including interfaces and access points. Compounding the situation is the fact that there can be many ways to access the data, multiple copies of the data, and data that is transmitted and/or stored *outside* of the database (backup tapes, third party systems, etc.).

From a threat perspective, the insider is widely considered to be the most dangerous, and for obvious reasons. He's already familiar with the environment, probably has a network logon ID, and is "trusted" by his coworkers and management. That's not to say that external threats ("hackers") should be ignored, but it's generally more difficult for such an individual to launch an attack since he must overcome external security mechanisms like the firewalls and intrusion detection/prevention systems (assuming those are in place and are configured appropriately).

The bottom line is this: do not rely too heavily on checklists. Do your research, ask the right questions, and look at what really matters.

## A Word About "Best Practices"

There are many "mainstream" security sources that make various (and sometimes conflicting) recommendations regarding Oracle database security. It is therefore critical that the auditor gather as much information as possible in order to ensure that all audit findings and recommendations are reasonable and take into account all relevant business and application requirements.

As always, the cost of implementing a recommendation must be balanced against its potential benefit(s).

# DATABASES

A **database** is a collection of data on disk in one or more files on a database server that collects and maintains related information.

- The **table** is the most important logical structure. Tables consist of:

  - Rows (tuples) and columns (attributes)

  - Files composing a database fall into two broad categories: database files and non-database files.

    - Database files contain data and metadata

    - Non-database files contain initialization parameters, logging information, and so forth.

# INSTANCES

- A **database** is stored on a server's hard disk; an **instance** exists in the server's memory.

- An Oracle instance is composed of a large block of memory called the System Global Area (SGA).

- Multiple instances can share the same database, and they usually reside on different servers.

- One purpose of using multiple instances is to have separate environments for production, QA and testing.

# VIEWS

A database **view** is a customized presentation of the data in a single table, or a join between two or more tables.

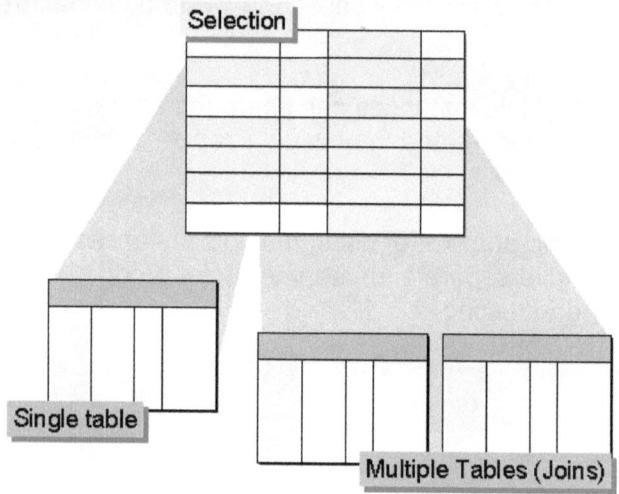

- Views contain no data themselves; the underlying query is run every time the view is accessed, and the results are presented to the user.

  - The underlying query cannot be viewed or modified by the user.

  - Views are commonly used as an access control mechanism to present only the information that the user is allowed to see.

# SCHEMA

The schema is basically the "layout" of a database, or the blueprint that outlines the way data is organized into tables.

It defines the tables, fields, relationships, views, procedures, functions, database links, directories, and other elements.

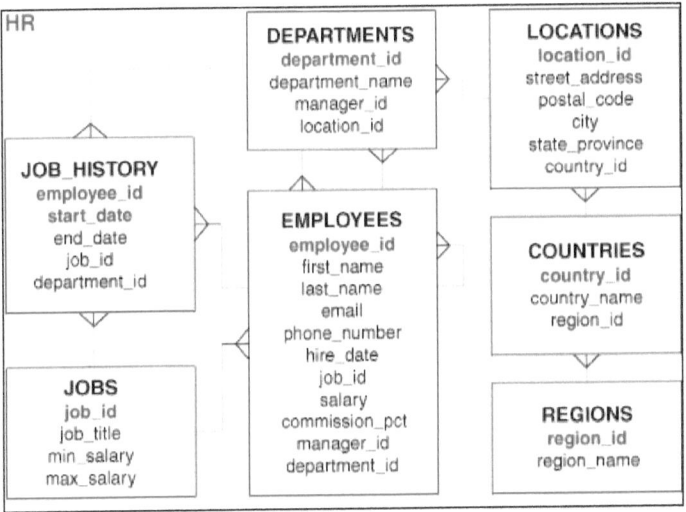

# NON-DATABASE SECURITY

- Usually there is an *oracle* account on the server where the Oracle software is installed.

  - It is common for the password to be "oracle", or something similar, so be sure to check for that.

- Ensure that backup media is secure.

- Verify that the permissions on the Oracle files and directories are appropriate.

- Check the appropriateness of the members of the **dba** and **oper** groups (Unix), or the **ORA_DBA** and **ORA_OPER** groups (Windows).

- Ensure that port 1521 (the default port for Oracle is not accessible directly from the Internet with no firewall or proxy server protection. Do the same for other ports that Oracle is using.

# MANAGING ORACLE

## *OEM*

Oracle Enterprise Manager (OEM) is a web-based administration interface.  It is accessed by typing

**http://<servername>:<port>/em** in a web browser.

For example: **http://myserver:5500/em**

By default, OEM runs on port 5500.  If it's not, check to see if it's running on another port.

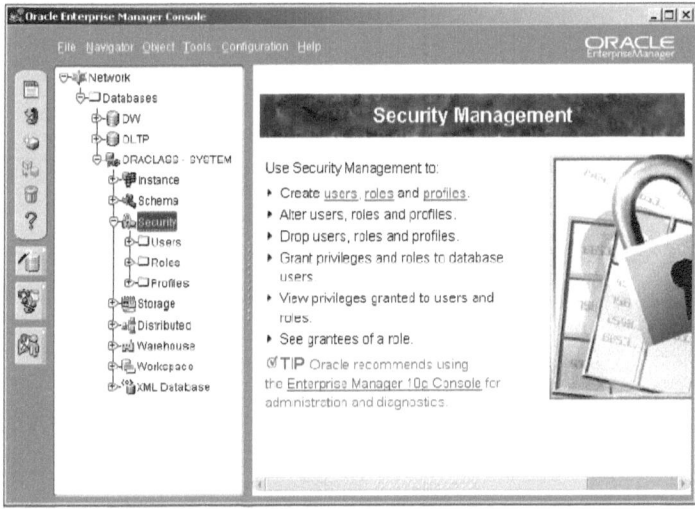

## *SQL*

- Structured Query Language (SQL) is a standard language for accessing and manipulating databases.

- Although SQL is an ANSI (American National Standards Institute) standard, there are many different versions of the SQL language. However, to be compliant with the ANSI standard, they all support at least the major commands (e.g. SELECT, UPDATE, DELETE, INSERT, WHERE) in a similar manner.

Example:

```
SQL> select Firstname,Lastname from
Employees
```

## PL/SQL

Procedural Language/SQL* extends SQL by adding constructs found in procedural languages, resulting in a structural language that is more powerful than SQL.

The following example will display "Hello World" 100 times, each on a separate line:

```
DECLARE
      i NUMBER:
BEGIN
      FOR i in 1..100 LOOP
DBMS_OUTPUT.PUT_LINE('Hello World');
      END LOOP;
END;
```

\* PL/SQL is a proprietary Oracle scripting language, similar to Transact-SQL (T-SQL) used by Microsoft SQL Server.

## SQL*PLUS

SQL*Plus is also heavily used. SQL*Plus is a command-line utility that can run SQL and PL/SQL commands, either interactively or from a script.

iSQLPlus is a web-based utility similar to the SQL*Plus command line utility for executing SQL and PL/SQL commands.

The default port for iSQLPlus is 5560.

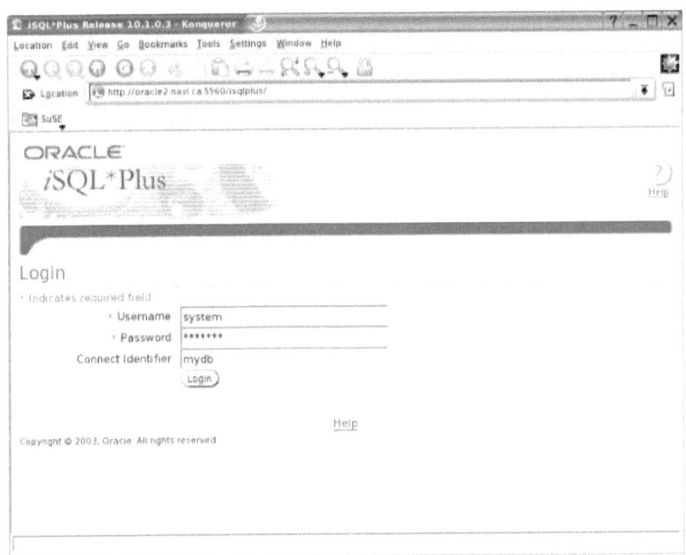

*Screenshot of iSQLPlus*

# CRITICAL FILES AND TABLES

Get the OS (Windows/UNIX) file permissions for the following types of files:

- Control (files and location in **v$controlfile** table)

- Datafiles (files and location in **v$datafile** table)

- The various **.ora** files (e.g., **init.ora**) – usually all the files in the Oracle Home directory *

- Check users with access to critical tables;

    - Example of critical system tables include dba_tab_privs; dba_objects; dba_users; v$parameter; sys.link$; sys.aud$.

\* The location of the Oracle home directory can usually be found in the /etc/oratab file.

# Users, Roles and Privileges

## *ADMINISTRATION CHECKS*

- Accounts must never be shared.

- The DBA and the system administrator should be different people.

- Operator and DBA responsibilities should be separated.

## *SHOWING THE ORACLE VERSION*

```
SQL> select * from v$version *
```

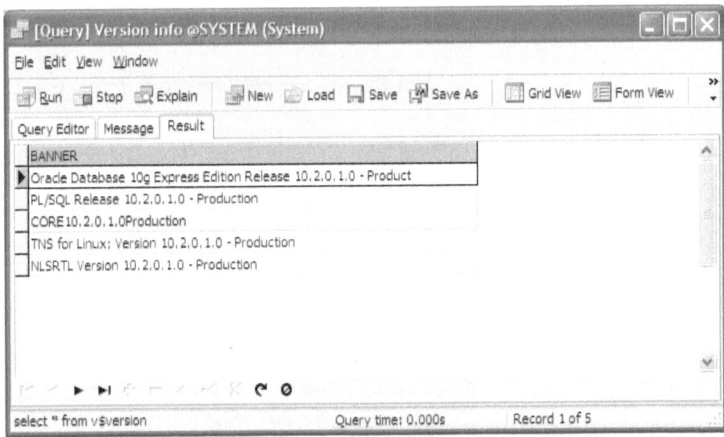

**The V$ table** is a generic term for a "virtual table" which allows the user to access memory structures within the SGA. V$ tables can be used to monitor the performance of processes within an Oracle instance. These tables are also called dynamic performance tables, because they are continuously updated while a database is open and in use.

## DATA DICTIONARY

- Contains all information about the structures and objects of the database such as tables, columns, users, data files etc. The data stored in the data dictionary are also often called *metadata*.

- The tables and views provided by the data dictionary contain information about:

    - users and their privileges

    - tables, table columns and their data types, integrity constraints, indexes

    - statistics about tables and indexes

    - privileges granted on database objects

    - storage structures of the database

    - Check the 07_DICTIONARY_ACCESSIBILITY parameter in the **init.ora** (also called the "pfile") file to see if set to FALSE. This prevents people with the 'select any table' privilege from selecting the data dictionary tables that may contain sensitive data such as encrypted passwords.

## BASIC ORACLE SECURITY CONCEPTS

- Parameters (Authentication, Audit Logging, etc.)

- Privileges

- Roles, which are simply named groups of privileges

- Profiles
    - Collection of settings that limits the use of system resources and the database

    - Table Permissions (Insert, Update, Delete, Select)

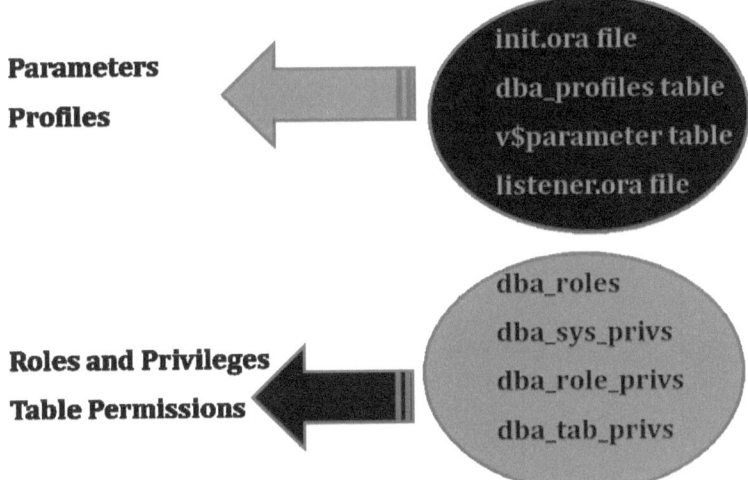

**Parameters**

**Profiles**

init.ora file

dba_profiles table

v$parameter table

listener.ora file

**Roles and Privileges**

**Table Permissions**

dba_roles

dba_sys_privs

dba_role_privs

dba_tab_privs

## SHOWING DEFAULT PARAMETER VALUES

SQL> SELECT Name, Value, ISDEFAULT FROM v$parameter ORDER BY name;

| Name | Value | ISDEFAULT |
|------|-------|-----------|
| 07_DICTIONARY_ACCESSIBILITY | TRUE | TRUE |
| audit_trail | NONE | TRUE |
| os_authent_prefix | OPS$ | TRUE |
| os_roles | FALSE | TRUE |
| remote_login_passwordfile | SHARED | FALSE |
| remote_os_authent | FALSE | TRUE |
| remote_os_roles | FALSE | TRUE |
| log_archive_start | FALSE | TRUE |

**Current Setting**

Alternatively, you can use the **show parameter** query to list ALL parameters.

Also, review the contents of the init.ora file.

## SHOWING DEFAULT PROFILE VALUES

SQL> select profile, resource_name, limit from dba_profiles;

| PROFILE | RESOURCE_NAME | LIMIT |
|---------|---------------|-------|
| DEFAULT | COMPOSITE_LIMIT | UNLIMITED |
| DEFAULT | FAILED_LOGIN_ATTEMPTS | 2 |
| DEFAULT | SESSIONS_PER_USER | UNLIMITED |
| DEFAULT | PASSWORD_LIFE_TIME | UNLIMITED |
| DEFAULT | CPU_PER_SESSION | UNLIMITED |
| DEFAULT | PASSWORD_REUSE_TIME | UNLIMITED |
| DEFAULT | CPU_PER_CALL | UNLIMITED |
| DEFAULT | PASSWORD_REUSE_MAX | UNLIMITED |
| DEFAULT | LOGICAL_READS_PER_SESSION | UNLIMITED |
| DEFAULT | PASSWORD_VERIFY_FUNCTION | UNLIMITED |
| DEFAULT | LOGICAL_READS_PER_CALL | UNLIMITED |
| DEFAULT | PASSWORD_LOCK_TIME | UNLIMITED |
| DEFAULT | IDLE_TIME | UNLIMITED |
| DEFAULT | PASSWORD_GRACE_TIME | UNLIMITED |
| DEFAULT | CONNECT_TIME | UNLIMITED |
| DEFAULT | PRIVATE_SGA | UNLIMITED |

16 rows selected.

- There are three ways users can be identified and authenticated in an Oracle database environment:

  - **Database Authentication**
    - User account and password exist within Oracle itself.

  - **Operating System Authentication**
    - The user's local server account or external LDAP (e.g. Active Directory) account is referenced. In this case, the account prefix is OPS$ (the default).
      - Oracle strongly recommends that **os_authent_prefix** be set to a null value (" ") for greater security.

      - Alternatively, an enterprise directory service such as Oracle Internet Directory (OID) can be referenced.

  - **Network Authentication**
    - Secure Sockets Layer (SSL)
    - Kerberos
    - Public Key Infrastructure (PKI)
    - Remote Authentication Dial-In User Interface (RADIUS)

17

## SYSTEM AND OBJECT PRIVILEGES

- After a user has been created, the user must be assigned the ability to log on to the database.

    - Once logged on, the user cannot perform any other tasks unless given the privilege to do so.

    - Most privileges are given to specific users or roles.

    - Role: named group of privileges that can be assigned to a user as a set rather than individually.

    - Two types of privileges:
        - System privileges
        - Object privileges


## USER AND RESOURCE CONTROL

- With a new DB instance, two users are created:
    - SYS
        - Owns most of the tables needed to run the DB, and data dictionary views
        - Owns a host of packages and procedures built into DB
        - Can perform high-level tasks (e.g., starting up and shutting down DB instance), and backup/recovery tasks

- The admin should not log on as SYS to perform routine tasks

- SYSTEM
  - Owns some tables, packages, and procedures

  - Has the DBA role: it can perform routine DB administration tasks

    - The SYSTEM account should be used to perform these routine tasks

## RECOMMENDED CONTROLS

- Create IDs for the DBAs and grant them DBA and SYSDBA privileges. When a user connects as SYSDBA he will have SYS privileges, but his activities can be tracked and tied to his ID.

- Lock the 'System' account.*

- The only time an admin should use SYS is to start/stop the database and grant privileges to v$ tables (explained later).

- Create strong passwords and change them on a regular basis, or when an administrator leaves the company.

In order to prevent a denial of service against SYS, Oracle has made it impossible to lock the SYS account by **failed_login_attempts.** However, this also means it is possible to brute force the password of the SYS account. It is possible to lock the SYS account explicitly by issuing the command "`alter user sys account lock`", but this does not stop someone from logging in as SYS with "as sysdba". Therefore, it is not really possible to lock out SYS.

*EXAMPLE: SHOWING ACCOUNT STATUS*

```
SQL> select username, account_status from dba_users;

USERNAME                      ACCOUNT_STATUS
----------------------------  ----------------
SYS                           OPEN
SYSTEM                        OPEN
OUTLN                         OPEN
DBSNMP                        OPEN
POS                           OPEN
AURORA$ORB$UNAUTHENTICATED    OPEN
SCOTT                         OPEN
DEMO                          EXPIRED/LOCKED
OPS$JOHNDOE                   OPEN

9 rows selected.
```

To list all user accounts and their attributes, run this query:

```
SQL> select * from all_users;
```

## *IDENTIFYING SYSTEM PRIVILEGES*

- SYSTEM has privileges needed for DBA activities.

- There are over 100 system privileges; for example:
    - SYSDBA
    - SYSOPER
    - SYSASM*
    - CREATE SESSION
    - CREATE TABLE and CREATE VIEW
    - CREATE USER
    - CREATE ANY TABLE
    - DROP ANY TABLE
    - SELECT ANY TABLE
    - GRANT ANY [OBJECT] PRIVILEGE
    - BACKUP ANY TABLE

* Only exists in Oracle 11g Release 1 (11.1), and is used to administer Automatic Storage Management (ASM).

## AUTHORIZATIONS

There are six major tables you can look at and cross-reference when determining who can do what in the database:

- DBA_USERS -- Lists the users
- DBA_ROLES -- Lists the roles
- DBA_ROLE_PRIVS -- Describes the roles granted to all users and roles in the database.
- DBA_COL_PRIVS -- describes all column object grants in the database.
- DBA_SYS_PRIVS -- describes system privileges granted to users and roles.
- DBA_TAB_PRIVS -- describes all object grants in the database.

## MAPPING ROLES AND PRIVILEGES

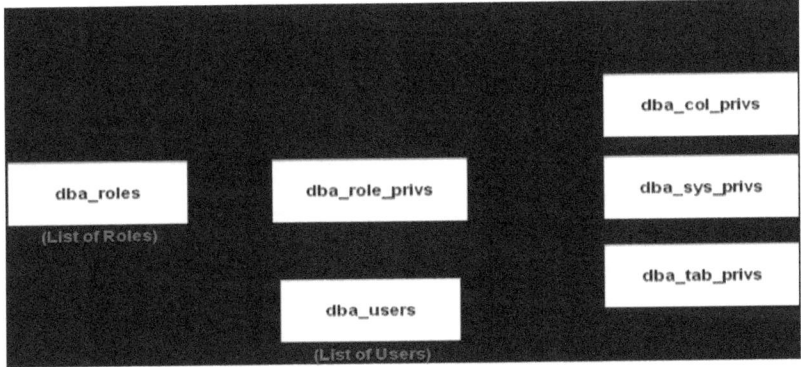

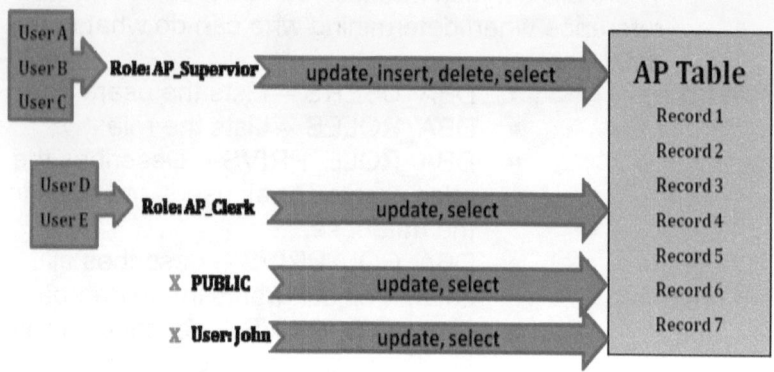

## PREDEFINED ROLES

Oracle provides some predefined roles to help in database administration. The major ones are listed below.

**CONNECT** - Includes the following system privileges: `ALTER SESSION`, `CREATE CLUSTER`, `CREATE DATABASE LINK`, `CREATE SEQUENCE`, `CREATE SESSION`, `CREATE SYNONYM`, `CREATE TABLE`, `CREATE VIEW`

**DBA** - All system privileges `WITH ADMIN OPTION`

**DELETE_CATALOG_ROLE** - Provides `DELETE` privilege on the system audit table (`AUD$`)

**HS_ADMIN_ROLE** - Used to protect access to the HS (Heterogeneous Services) data dictionary tables (grants SELECT) and packages (grants EXECUTE). It is granted to SELECT_CATALOG_ROLE and EXECUTE_CATALOG_ROLE such that users with generic data dictionary access also can access the HS data dictionary.

**EXECUTE_CATALOG_ROLE** - Provides EXECUTE privilege on objects in the data dictionary. Also, has the HS_ADMIN_ROLE.

**EXP_FULL_DATABASE** - Provides the privileges required to perform full and incremental database exports. Includes: SELECT ANY TABLE, BACKUP ANY TABLE, EXECUTE ANY PROCEDURE, EXECUTE ANY TYPE, ADMINISTER RESOURCE MANAGER, and INSERT, DELETE, and UPDATE on the tables SYS.INCVID, SYS.INCFIL, and SYS.INCEXP. Also has the following roles: EXECUTE_CATALOG_ROLE and SELECT_CATALOG_ROLE.

**IMP_FULL_DATABASE** - Provides the privileges required to perform full database imports. Includes an extensive list of system privileges (use view DBA_SYS_PRIVS to view privileges) and the following roles: EXECUTE_CATALOG_ROLE and SELECT_CATALOG_ROLE.

**RESOURCE** - Includes the following system privileges: CREATE CLUSTER, CREATE INDEXTYPE, CREATE OPERATOR, CREATE PROCEDURE, CREATE SEQUENCE, CREATE TABLE, CREATE TRIGGER, CREATE TYPE

**SELECT_CATALOG_ROLE** - Provides SELECT privilege on objects in the data dictionary. Also has the HS_ADMIN_ROLE.

## EXAMPLE: LISTING PRIVILEGES

```
SQL> select * from dba_role_privs;
```

| GRANTEE | GRANTED_ROLE | ADM | DEF |
|---|---|---|---|
| DBA | DELETE_CATALOG_ROLE | YES | YES |
| DBA | EXECUTE_CATALOG_ROLE | YES | YES |
| DBA | EXP_FULL_DATABASE | NO | YES |
| DBA | IMP_FULL_DATABASE | NO | YES |
| DBA | SELECT_CATALOG_ROLE | YES | YES |
| DBSNMP | CONNECT | NO | YES |
| DBSNMP | RESOURCE | NO | YES |
| DBSNMP | SNMPAGENT | NO | YES |
| DEMO | CONNECT | NO | YES |
| DEMO | RESOURCE | NO | YES |
| EXP_FULL_DATABASE | EXECUTE_CATALOG_ROLE | NO | YES |
| EXP_FULL_DATABASE | SELECT_CATALOG_ROLE | NO | YES |
| IMP_FULL_DATABASE | EXECUTE_CATALOG_ROLE | NO | YES |
| IMP_FULL_DATABASE | SELECT_CATALOG_ROLE | NO | YES |
| JAVADEBUGPRIV | JAVAUSERPRIV | NO | YES |
| JAVASYSPRIV | JAVADEBUGPRIV | NO | YES |

*EXAMPLE: LISTING PRIVILEGES FOR A SPECIFIC ROLE*

```
SQL> select * from role_sys_privs where role = 'IMP_FULL_DATABASE' order by 1,2;
```

| ROLE | PRIVILEGE | ADM |
|------|-----------|-----|
| IMP_FULL_DATABASE | ADMINISTER DATABASE TRIGGER | NO |
| IMP_FULL_DATABASE | ADMINISTER RESOURCE MANAGER | NO |
| IMP_FULL_DATABASE | ALTER ANY PROCEDURE | NO |
| IMP_FULL_DATABASE | ALTER ANY TABLE | NO |
| IMP_FULL_DATABASE | ALTER ANY TRIGGER | NO |
| IMP_FULL_DATABASE | ALTER ANY TYPE | NO |
| IMP_FULL_DATABASE | ANALYZE ANY | NO |
| IMP_FULL_DATABASE | AUDIT ANY | NO |
| IMP_FULL_DATABASE | BECOME USER | NO |
| IMP_FULL_DATABASE | COMMENT ANY TABLE | NO |
| IMP_FULL_DATABASE | CREATE ANY TABLE | NO |
| IMP_FULL_DATABASE | CREATE ANY CLUSTER | NO |
| IMP_FULL_DATABASE | CREATE ANY CONTEXT | NO |
| IMP_FULL_DATABASE | CREATE ANY DIMENSION | NO |
| IMP_FULL_DATABASE | CREATE ANY DIRECTORY | NO |

*ADMIN OPTION*

- On the previous page, you may have noticed the third column had a heading of 'ADM'. This parameter is used to delegate administrative responsibilities to other users. However, many companies view this as a security risk (and rightly so!) so they prohibit this option from being used.

- Privileges that are granted WITH ADMIN OPTION can be passed to other users. When this is the case, the value of ADM will be 'YES'.

26

- Example of user 'John' being granted the CREATE TABLE privilege, with the ability to grant it to other users:

      GRANT
        CREATE TABLE
      TO
        John
      WITH ADMIN OPTION;

## ADMINISTRATIVE PRIVILEGES

Review all users that have the following privileges (query the 'dba_sys_privs' table):

```
CREATE USER
CREATE ROLE
ALTER USER
ALTER ANY ROLE
DROP USER
DROP ANY ROLE
GRANT ANY PRIVILEGE
GRANT ANY ROLE
```

Any OS level accounts that DBAs use should be individual accounts – the account that owns the Oracle files should be locked at the OS level.

# EXAMPLE: LISTING ADMINISTRATIVE PRIVILEGES

```
SQL> SELECT grantee, privilege, admin_option
  2  FROM dba_sys_privs
  3  WHERE (privilege = 'CREATE USER' or
  4  privilege = 'CREATE ROLE' or
  5  privilege = 'ALTER USER' or
  6  privilege = 'ALTER ANY ROLE' or
  7  privilege = 'DROP USER' or
  8  privilege = 'DROP ANY ROLE' or
  9  privilege = 'GRANT ANY PRIVILEGE' or
 10  privilege = 'GRANT ANY ROLE')
 11  ORDER BY grantee;
```

| GRANTEE | PRIVILEGE | ADM |
|---|---|---|
| DBA | ALTER ANY ROLE | YES |
| DBA | ALTER USER | YES |
| DBA | CREATE ROLE | YES |
| DBA | CREATE USER | YES |
| DBA | DROP ANY ROLE | YES |
| DBA | DROP USER | YES |
| DBA | GRANT ANY PRIVILEGE | YES |
| DBA | GRANT ANY ROLE | YES |
| IMP_FULL_DATABASE | CREATE ROLE | NO |
| IMP_FULL_DATABASE | CREATE USER | NO |
| IMP_FULL_DATABASE | DROP ANY ROLE | NO |
| IMP_FULL_DATABASE | DROP USER | NO |

12 rows selected.

# PUBLIC ROLE

PUBLIC is like the default group 'Everyone' in Windows.  All database users inherit privileges given to PUBLIC.  In general, privileges of PUBLIC should be limited.  The following areas should be queried:

- System Privileges (i.e., privileges other than to create a database session) – review the **dba_sys_privs** table.
- Object/Table Privileges – review the **dba_tab_privs** table.
- Specific Column Privileges – review the **dba_col_privs** table.

- There are two areas of concern regarding default grants to PUBLIC:

  - Access to data dictionary views
    - Example: ALL_USERS view
  - Execute on procedures
    - Example: UTL_SMTP, UTL_HTTP, UTL_TCP, UTL_FILE *

- Care should be taken so nothing "breaks"
  - Applications may need certain PUBLIC privileges, so you need to understand application dependencies.

## *SHOW PRIVILEGES GRANTED TO PUBLIC*

```
SQL> SELECT grantee, owner, table_name, privilege FROM
dba_tab_privs WHERE grantee = 'PUBLIC' ORDER BY
table_name,privilege,grantee;


GRANTEE   OWNER  TABLE_NAME                       PRIVILEGE
------------------------------------------------------------
PUBLIC    SYS    /ec7484c4_byteArrayHolder        EXECUTE
PUBLIC    SYS    /ec7e6354_Property               EXECUTE
PUBLIC    SYS    /ec97e8aa_SmartTcpListener       EXECUTE
PUBLIC    SYS    /eca21049_OracleResourceLocati   EXECUTE
PUBLIC    SYS    /eca898fe_Main                   EXECUTE
PUBLIC    SYS    /ecc3b2ea_ResolutionDriver       EXECUTE
```

The query below does the same thing, except it queries the DBA_COL_PRIVS table:

```
SQL> SELECT grantee, owner, column_name, table_name,
privilege FROM dba_col_privs WHERE grantee = 'PUBLIC'
ORDER BY table_name, column_name, privilege, grantee;
```

# LISTING ROLES IN OEM

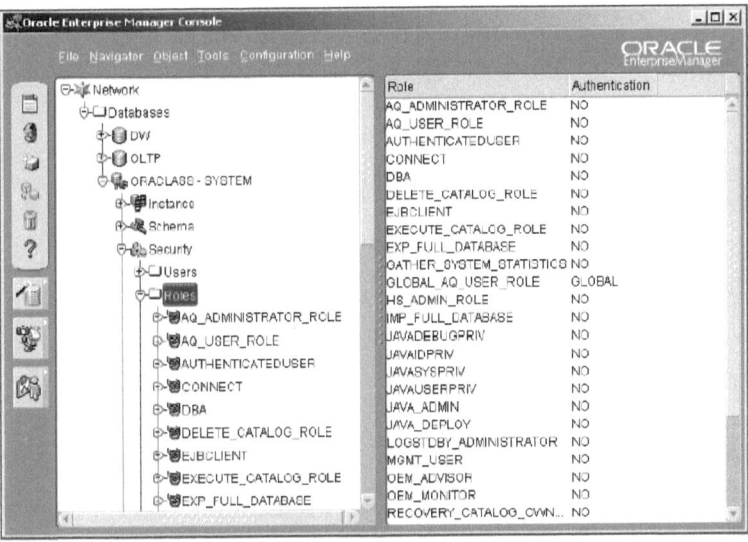

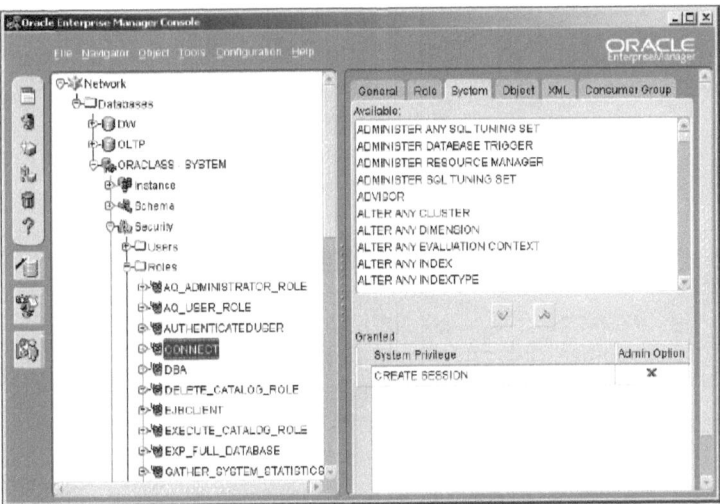

# ENCRYPTION

Encryption capabilities within Oracle databases have progressively improved with each version. Oracle 9i introduced row level encryption, and Oracle 10g introduced row and column encryption.

- To ensure that all client connections to the database are encrypted (e.g., protect the confidentiality of the password), the parameter ORA_ENCRYPT_LOGIN should be set to TRUE on the client machine.

- One or more columns of data can be encrypted as necessary.

  - Oracle 10g Release 1 and earlier use the DBMS_CRYPTO and DBMS_OBFUSCATION_TOOLKIT toolkits. Some programming skill is required to use these.

  - Oracle 10g Release 2 and later use Transparent Data Encryption (TDE). This allows admins to implement encryption right out of the box without having to write code. In addition, encryption of entire tablespaces can be performed.

Data *masking* can also be performed. Data masking is different from encryption in that sensitive data (e.g. social security numbers, salary information) is "scrubbed" in order to share that data with development/test, analysis groups, business partners, etc.

- The OEM (Oracle Enterprise Manager) Data Masking Pack is a separate product that uses an irreversible process to replace sensitive data with realistic looking, but scrubbed, data based on masking rules. This ensures that original data cannot be retrieved, recovered or restored. OEM version 10.2.0.4. is required to use it.

In this example, the last name and SSN data is masked, but the salary data is preserved.

| LAST_NAME | SSN | SALARY |
|-----------|-----|--------|
| Johnson | 203-40-2324 | 80,000 |
| Adams | 323-33-9793 | 87,000 |
| Williams | 324-56-2067 | 67,000 |
| Kawalski | 204-66-6935 | 76,000 |

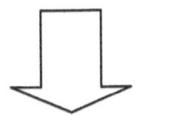 

| LAST_NAME | SSN | SALARY |
|-----------|-----|--------|
| Kghkehh | 111-11-4959 | 80,000 |
| Ihwoiherkjeo | 111-22-6843 | 87,000 |
| Oiwenrhiowo | 111-56-3985 | 67,000 |
| Bhihwewni | 111-55-5683 | 76,000 |

- Alternatively, the DBA could use PL/SQL to implement a sort of "poor man's" masking solution. For example:

  1. Bulk load "employee data" into a PL/SQL table,

  2. In the PL/SQL table, shift column "last_name" one row up, column first_name one row down

# AUDITING PASSWORDS

## *PASSWORD MANAGEMENT*

- If an application is relied upon for authentication, gain an understanding of how the process works. Are passwords encrypted? Is there a password minimum length? What are the composition rules? Where are the passwords stored?

- Oracle 10g maintains passwords in encrypted format in the **DBA_USERS** table. An account must have either admin access to show this information, or it must have the SELECT ANY TABLE and/or SELECT ANY DICTIONARY privilege.

    **This last statement is CRITICAL. Do not assume that just because an account does not have DBA privileges that it can't access the password hashes. If any account has SELECT ANY TABLE and/or SELECT ANY DICTIONARY privilege then it can access those hashes!**

- In 11g, the password hashes are located in the "SPARE4" column of the **SYS.USER$** table.

- Review the **DBA_PROFILES** table for the default profiles for password parameters related to expiration, lock out, quality verification, etc.

- Run a password strength check (query) to make sure that passwords conform to policy. Two examples are **cracker-v2.0.sql** and **woraauthbf**, both of which are freely available on the Internet.

## DBA_PROFILES TABLE

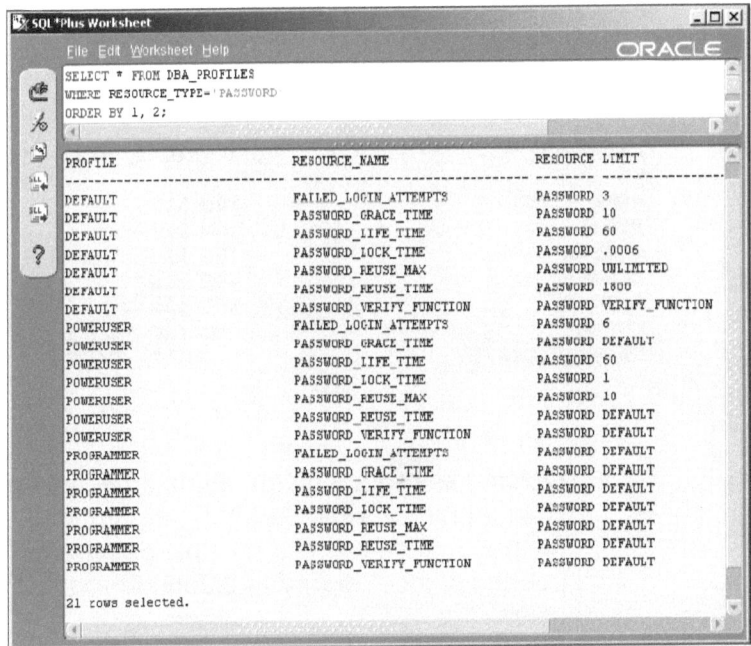

- Oracle Password SecurityPasswords are encrypted with the DES algorithm, while Oracle 11g uses the SHA-1 algorithm.

    - Query the **DBA_USERS** table and look at the values in the "password_versions" column to determine which encryption mechanism applies to each user's password, as shown below.

```
SQL> SELECT username, password_versions AS versions, FROM
dba_users;

USERNAME                                VERSIONS
-----------------------------------     --------
MGMT_VIEW                               10G 11G
SYS                                     10G 11G
SYSTEM                                  10G 11G
DBSNMP                                  10G 11G
SYSMAN                                  10G 11G
OUTLN                                   10G 11G
FLOWS_FILES                             10G 11G
```

- Oracle password security is implemented via Oracle profiles, which are then assigned to users. This means that multiple password policies can be applied to different groups of users.

- As of Oracle 11g, database passwords are case sensitive. This can be disabled by setting the SEC_CASE_SENSITIVE_LOGON initialization parameter to FALSE (the default is TRUE). As an auditor, you should check this parameter to ensure it is line with your company's security policy.

- When an older version of an Oracle database is migrated to Oracle 11g, the existing user passwords will remain **case-insensitive** until users change them!

## DEFAULT IDS AND PASSWORDS

- SCOTT/TIGER,
- DBSNMP/DBSNMP,
- SYSTEM/MANAGER,
- SYS/CHANGE_ON_INSTALL,
- TRACESVR/TRACE,
- CTXSYS/CTXSYS,
- MDSYS/MDSYS,
- DEMO/DEMO,
- CTXDEMO/CTXDEMO,
- APPLSYS/FND,
- PO8/PO8,
- JONES/STEEL
- CLARK/CLOTH

- NAMES/NAMES,
- SYSADM/SYSADM,
- ORDPLUGINS/ORDPLUGINS,
- OUTLN/OUTLN,
- APPS/APPS
- DBAADVANTAGE/DBAADVANTAGE
- READONLY/READONLY
- INTERNAL/INTERNAL
- ADAMS/WOOD
- BLAKE/PAPER
- AURORA$ORB$UNAUTHENTICATED/INVALID
- INTERNAL/ORACLE
- SAP/SAPR3 (for SAP only)

Over **140** default username/passwords have been collected from the field, including application accounts for packages such as Peoplesoft and Hyperion!

In Oracle 11g, the easy way to identify accounts with default passwords is to have the DBA run the following query:

```
SELECT * FROM DBA_USERS_WITH_DEFPWD;
```

To find both the names of accounts that have default passwords, and the status of those accounts, have the DBA perform the following:

```
SELECT d.username, u.account_status
FROM DBA_USERS_WITH_DEFPWD d, DBA_USERS u
WHERE d.username = u.username
ORDER BY 2,1;
```

Query the **user_password_limits** view to display the password profile parameters that are assigned to the user.

The default limits for a 10g R2 database are:

```
RESOURCE_NAME                        LIMIT
------------------------------------ ----------
FAILED_LOGIN_ATTEMPTS                10
PASSWORD_LIFE_TIME                   UNLIMITED
PASSWORD_REUSE_TIME                  UNLIMITED
PASSWORD_REUSE_MAX                   UNLIMITED
PASSWORD_VERIFY_FUNCTION             NULL
PASSWORD_LOCK_TIME                   UNLIMITED
PASSWORD_GRACE_TIME                  UNLIMITED
```

The default limits for an 11g database are:

```
RESOURCE_NAME                        LIMIT
------------------------------------ ----------
FAILED_LOGIN_ATTEMPTS                10
PASSWORD_LIFE_TIME                   180
PASSWORD_REUSE_TIME                  UNLIMITED
PASSWORD_REUSE_MAX                   UNLIMITED
PASSWORD_VERIFY_FUNCTION             NULL
PASSWORD_LOCK_TIME                   1
PASSWORD_GRACE_TIME                  7
```

# EXAMPLE: *USER_PASSWORD_LIMITS*

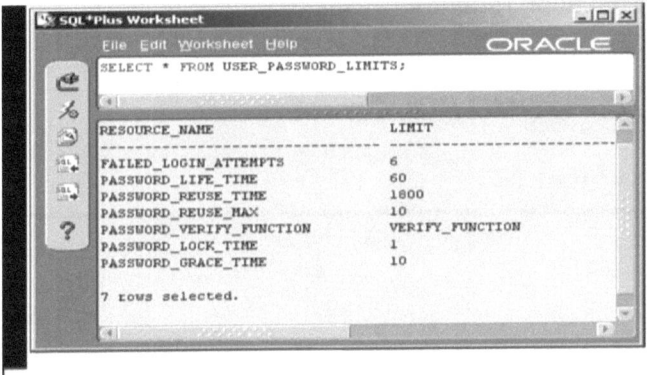

## ENFORCING PASSWORD QUALITY

Oracle's password complexity verification routine can be specified using a PL/SQL script called **utlpwdmg.sql**, which sets the default profile parameters .

The password complexity check is NOT enabled by default.  In order to enable it, the PASSWORD_VERIFY_FUNCTION option must be set to verify_function, verify_function_11g, or a custom function (see previous page).

Examine the *password_verify_function* option in the **DBA_PROFILES** table to see what the value is set to.

The *utlpwdmg.sql* was updated in Oracle 11g to include stronger settings.

Remember that DBAs can customize the **utlpwdmg.sql** script to create their own enhanced verification routines.

## *UTLPWDMG.SQL DEFAULTS*

| Oracle 10g | Oracle 11g |
|---|---|
| Minimum length of 4 | Minimum length of 8 |
| Not the same as the userid | Same as 10g, plus it is not the user name spelled backward or with numeric characters appended. In addiiton, it is not the same as the server name or the server name with the numbers 1–100 appended. |
| At least one alpha and one numeric character | Same. However, 11g supports mixed-case letters, as well as special characters such as punctuation marks. |
| Does not match simple words like welcome, account, database, or user. | Same as 10g, plus it is not welcome1, database1, account1, user1234, password1, oracle, oracle123, etc. |
| Differs from the previous password by at least 3 letters | Same |
| PASSWORD_VERIFY_FUNCTION = `verify_function` | PASSWORD_VERIFY_FUNCTION = `verify_function_11g` |

# REMOTE ACCESS

- If username and password are included in a script (e.g., sqlplus, application, etc.), there is a potential security hole that somebody unauthorized may view it (e.g., ps command in UNIX may enumerate the password).

- If there are OPS$ (or other designated prefix) accounts, and the REMOTE_OS_AUTHENT parameter is set to 'TRUE', then the account will bypass database authentication (no password required).

- Generally, it's better not to allow REMOTE_OS_AUTHENT

  - Note that the REMOTE_OS_AUTHENT parameter has been deprecated in Oracle 11g.

## ORAPWD

Orapwd is a utility for creating a password file for authenticating users. The contents of this file are encrypted, and the file cannot be read directly.

Check V$PWFILE_USERS to see who has OSDBA/OSOPER access.

Operating system authentication takes precedence over password file authentication.

The remote_login_password parameter determines how the password file will be utilized:

- None: No password file is used. Only OS-authenticated users can perform privileged tasks.
- Exclusive: password file can be used only by one database.
- Shared: allows more than one database to use password file.

## LISTENER

- Listener is a utility that 'listens' for database connection requests.

- Default listener port is 1521; nobody should be able to access this from the Internet!

- The *listener.ora* file should be protected as passwords *might* be in clear text.

- Local administration of the listener is secure by default through the local operating system. Therefore configuring a password is neither required nor recommended for secure local administration.

- In Oracle Database 11g Release 2 (11.2), the password feature is being deprecated. This does not cause a loss of security because authentication is enforced through local operating system authentication.

- A password is required for remote listener administration, that is, when the listener control utility is installed on a remote computer.

- If the client is administering the listener remotely over an insecure network and they require maximum security, they need to configure the listener communication with SSL 9Secure Sockets Layer).

.

## DATABASE LINKS

Database Links provides a mechanism to connect to another instance of a database without the worry of where and how the data resides on the other database.  This allows a user to access data from multiple databases as one data source.
How to audit:

- It can be difficult to determine what databases have created links into another database without reviewing other databases (ask DBA and/or App. Manager on the use of db links).

- Review the contents of the **DBA_DB_LINKS** table for existence of links to other databases. If db links exist, inquire about the nature, use and need of such links (data integrity issue – not a big security issue for the database being reviewed).

- Usually there is no need for 'PUBLIC' to own any db links.

- **Use commands** "select * from dba_db_links" **and** "select * from user_db_links"

# AUDIT FEATURES

## *AUDITING*

- Regardless of whether database auditing is enabled, Oracle always audits certain database-related operations and writes them to the operating system audit file. This is called **mandatory auditing**, and it includes the following operations:
    - Connections to the instance with administrator privileges (any user connecting to Oracle as SYSOPER or SYSDBA).
    - Database startup
    - Database shutdown

- Mandatory auditing events, by default, are written to the Windows event log, or to the *adump* directory on Unix.

- The parameter AUDIT_TRAIL controls the format and location of audit log files.
    - Bear in mind that when the value of this parameter is changed, the database must be shut down and restarted for the change to take effect.
    - The role DELETE_CATALOG_ROLE is provided for use with a special account in a batch job to archive and truncate the audit table.

- Auditing parameter defaults:
    - Disabled in Oracle 10g (AUDIT_TRAIL = NONE)
    - Enabled in Oracle 11g (AUDIT_TRAIL = DB)

## AUDIT LOG LOCATIONS

| Value of AUDIT_TRAIL parameter | Action |
| --- | --- |
| NONE, FALSE | Disable auditing |
| OS | Enable auditing. Send audit records to an operating system file. |
| DB, TRUE | Enable auditing. Send audit records to the SYS.AUD$ table. |
| DB_EXTENDED | Enable auditing. Send audit records to the SYS.AUD$ table, and record additional informaiton in the CLOB columns SQLBIND and SQLTEXT. |
| XML | Enable auditing and write all records in XML format. |
| EXTENDED | Enable auditing and record all columns in the audit trail, including SqlText and SqlBind values. |

## STANDARD AUDITING

Standard Auditing consists of three different auditing categories that can be run by Oracle automatically:

- Statement auditing
- Privilege auditing
- Object auditing

Auditing commands have no effect until the administrator sets the AUDIT_TRAIL initialization parameter:

- Modify the init.ora file
- Log file is stored in the AUD$ table.


- Data dictionary views you can query for audit trail results:

  - DBA_AUDIT_EXISTS

- DBA_AUDIT_OBJECT
- DBA_AUDIT_SESSION
- DBA_AUDIT_STATEMENT
- DBA_AUDIT_TRAIL

- The above metadata views have a corresponding USER_counterpart, except for DBA_AUDIT_EXISTS

## AUDITING USERS AND PRIVILEGES

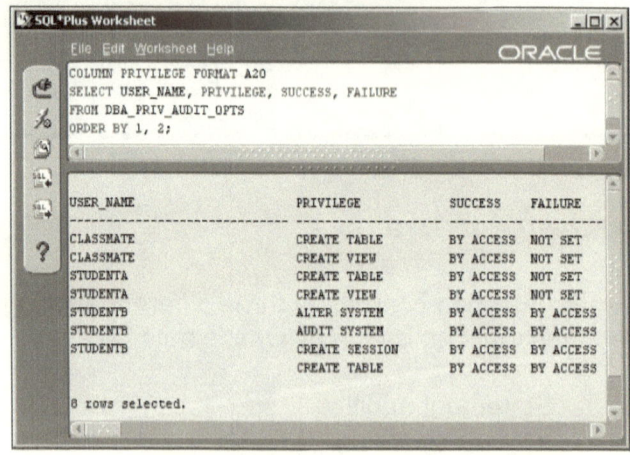

## EXAMPLE: SHOWING AUDIT PARAMETERS

```
SQL> SHOW PARAMETER AUDIT
NAME                    TYPE      VALUE
------------------------------- ----------- ---------
---------------------
AUDIT_FILE_DEST   STRING   C:\ORACLE\PRODUCT\10.2.0\ADMIN
\DB10G\ADUMP
AUDIT_SYS_OPERATIONS     BOOLEAN  FALSE
AUDIT_TRAIL              STRING   NONE
SQL>
```

### WHAT IS BEING AUDITED?

- There are three views that show you what the current standard audit settings are:

  - DBA_STMT_AUDIT_OPTS shows the statement auditing settings.

```
select * from dba_stmt_audit_opts;
```

  - DBA_PRIV_AUDIT_OPTS shows the privilege auditing settings.

```
select * from dba_priv_audit_opts;
```

  - DBA_OBJ_AUDIT_OPTS shows the object auditing settings.

```
select * from dba_priv_audit_opts;
```

### PROTECTING THE AUDIT TRAIL

Any non-SYS user can access the audit trail if he is a member of the DELETE_ANY_CATALOG role, so check for that.

The administrator can audit access to the audit trail by running the following command:

SQL> audit all on sys.aud$ by access;

If audit records are deleted then another row will be added that will show that the rows were deleted.

An additional control is that if AUDIT_SYS_OPERATIONS is set to TRUE, then any sessions using **as sysdba**, **as sysoper**, or connecting as SYS itself will be logged in the operating system audit location.

## *Fine-Grained Auditing (FGA)*

Introduced in oracle 9i, FGA provides the capability to audit specific rows and columns within a table. This is accomplished using the DBMS_FGA package.

Using FGA ...

- The event handler can alert an administrator to a triggering condition (e.g. write record to log, send an email)

- Audit records are stored in the FGA_LOG$ table, not the AUD$ table

- Audit data can be written out to XML-format files for additional security

- FGA is completely independent of the AUDIT_TRAIL parameter

Here is a basic example of FGA in action. This policy audits any queries of salaries greater than $150,000.

```
BEGIN
 DBMS_FGA.add_policy(
   object_schema    => 'AUDIT_TEST',
   object_name      => 'PAYROLL',
   policy_name      => 'SALARY_CHK_AUDIT',
   audit_condition => 'SALARY > 150000',
   audit_column     => 'SALARY');
END;
```

Note: **object_name** in this case refers to a table named "PAYROLL"

Interestingly, the DBA can also create and associate one or more procedures that will execute if the audit event condition is met. Fo rexample:

```
BEGIN
 DBMS_FGA.add_policy(
   object_schema   => 'AUDITOR',
   object_name     => 'PAYROLL',
   policy_name     => 'SALARY_CHK_AUDIT',
   audit_condition => 'SALARY > 150000',
   audit_column    => 'SALARY');
   handler_schema  => 'AUDITOR');
   handler_module  => 'LOCK_ACCOUNT');
END;
```

In this case, a procedure called "LOCK_ACCOUNT" has been defined that will lock out any account that performs a query (i.e. runs a 'SELECT' statement) against the PAYROLL table to view employees with salaries over $150,000.

Of course, FGA can also be used to detect other actions such as UPDATE, INSERT, and DELETE.


## *Oracle Audit Vault*

Oracle Audit Vault (not to be confused with Database Vault) automates the audit event collection, monitoring and reporting process. As of the date of this writing, the latest release of Oracle Audit Vault is 10.2.3.2. This version supports monitoring Microsoft SQL Server 2000, 2005, and 2008, IBM DB2 UDB 8.2 through 9.5, Sybase ASE 12.5.4 through 15.0.x databases.

Oracle Audit Vault is a separate product that requires two licenses: one license for the Audit Vault server; and one or more licenses for each of the Audit Vault agents.